DRINKING GAMES 2000

Down Down

TAKE THAT BOOKS

Take That Ltd.
P.O.Box 200
Harrogate
HG1 2YR
Fax:01423-526035
Email: sales@takethat.co.uk
www.takethat.co.uk

Cartoons by Joe Mckeough

10 9 8 7 6 5 4 3 2 1

Layout and typesetting by Take That Ltd.,
P.O.Box 200, Harrogate, HG1 2YR.
Previously published as 99 Drinking Games

Printed and bound in Great Britain.

ISBN 1-873668-22-8

TAKE THAT BOOKS

Why?

Nobody needs an incentive to drink beer. That would be like saying you need a bribe to keep on breathing. But the act of imbibing alcoholic fluids **can** become somewhat tedious. After exhausting all possible subjects of conversation, including football, religion and politics you sometimes grind to a halt. Should you just sit there and continue to drink, as is your duty? Or should you look for ways of livening up the experience? The same applies to parties. Once you've had a bit of a dance, browsed through the host's CD collection and been rejected by all the available members of the opposite sex, you need a way to have fun.

Drinking games offer the perfect solution for both of these scenarios. They don't have to be played with beer, or even alcoholic drinks (but they tend to be more fun that way). All you need are a group of willing participants, a ready supply of drinks and a sense of humour.

Enjoy!

Down Down

Warning

This bit is serious

Drinking large amounts of alcohol can be dangerous. Everyone has a different limit, you know yours and you shouldn't exceed it even if provoked by your peers. Every year hundreds, yes hundreds, of people die from alcohol abuse. A significant proportion of those deaths can be attributed to one binge. So, please stop before you do yourself harm - there's nothing clever about being dead and it severely limits your ability to have fun.

Drinking and driving is also extremely dangerous and likely to be deadly. Any amounts of alcohol, no matter how long you've been drinking and how big you are, will slow your reflexes and impair your judgement. Apart from risking your licence, you are increasing the chances of killing yourself, or even worse, murdering someone else. There may be a 'legal limit' for the amount of alcohol you can have in your blood when driving, but we recommend that you simply don't mix the two. If you are going to play these games with alcohol, please designate a driver who will only drink softies (and don't tempt them), use taxis or get a bus.

Rules & Etiquette

While the games listed in this tome all include a list of basic rules and accompanying forfeits, feel completely free to alter them at will. Indeed, some of the best laughs come at the beginning of festivities when you create 'house' rules and take a vote on the penalties. The rule with rules is that they are directly proportional to the amount that will be consumed.

Etiquette, on the other hand is a matter for Government and the following should be strictly adhered to. Any persistent violations will result in the offending parties being pulled in front of the Drinking Games Court. Be warned that the adjudicating panel consist of the twelve most infamous drinking games exponents in the world - a group not to be messed with. There is no right of appeal.

No saying the word, "Drink"
Imbibe, partake of the fluid, hoist one, get it down, or slam it, but never, ever drink! (see page 65).

No Pointing with Fingers

Since most of the fun in drinking games comes from others' failings this point is often violated. The most common substitute is to use your elbow to indicate direction.

No Hats in the Circle

Headgear is not permitted in any game unless specifically called for by the rules.

Wrong Hands

Right handers should drink with their left hand and vice-versa. Ask players to sign a registration form to allow their participation and establish their usual hand. Note: anybody signing in with anything other than an 'X' must sink one.

No swearing

F@#*ing hard to stick too, but a point of etiquette nevertheless. The sensible object behind this is to remove the easiest objection from anybody disapproving of your activities.

Discreet Digit

At any point, in any of the games, anybody can discreetly drop their hand below the playing surface, leaving a single index finger on top. When they notice, other players must copy. The last the realise bungs one down the throat.

No Pronouns

Personal, interrogative or possessive - they're all banned!

Hold 'em

Most games include a hierarchy. When addressing God, The King, President or Leader, you must firmly grasp your (*own*) nuts or breast with your drinking hand.

"You have been warned!"

What is a Drink?

Getting it exactly 'right' is the job of the most experienced gamer at any gathering - and the definition of 'right' lies somewhere between sobriety and unconsciousness. Therefore, it is down to the participating group to decide what constitutes a "drink".

Clearly a bawdy gang of 18 stone builders will have a greater tolerance than your average knitting circle! So where the former might down a couple of gallons for the meekest of offences, the latter may just sniff the fumes.

Here are some generally accepted volumes...

The Finger

The 'finger' is the accepted standard measure of drinking games and can easily be regulated.. Pick up your glass and place your uppermost finger so that the top is level with the top of your drink. Now consume enough fluid to bring the level down to the underside of your finger. For two drinks, either repeat this process or put two fingers together on the glass and drink to the bottom of the second. The beauty of this measurement system is that generally bigger people, who can drink more, have larger fingers!

A Half Pint or Full Can

This is quite a hefty measure and should only be used for low penalty games to increase the Blitz Factor. Don't even contemplate it if you are using anything stronger than beer. Easy to regulate.

A Sip or Mouthful

A very difficult measure to regulate and open to abuse by those wishing to get really blitzed or stay sober. Ironically it is that precise reason which makes it a popular game volume, leaving the players to judge their own progress. Ideal for games played with spirits.

Three Swallows

A nice middle-of-the-road quantity for use with beer. Allows a certain amount of self-regulation whilst allowing other players to witness the number of swallows.

30 ml/1 fl oz

The volume of choice for drinking game aficionados. However the precision required to line up a new drink makes it almost impossible to use in fast moving games, particularly after a few rounds.

Shot Glass

Obviously designed for games with liquids stronger than ordinary beer. Double shots, however, do make good amber nectar vessels.

Small Cup

A popular measure for parties and home games. Gives a good degree of regulation, allows a certain amount of flexibility to suit individual players and is easily available.

Board Games

Adapted For The Cause

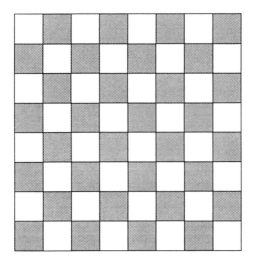

Beergammon

Blitz Factor 2

A game for two, based on the board game Backgammon. Fairly easy to play but the Blitz Factor can increase rapidly if you are up against a Backgammon expert.

How to Play:

Play a game of Backgammon in the normal way, with one player taking the white pieces and one player taking the black or red. Each time one of your pieces is taken off the board and placed on the bar you must take a drink. Also, in the end game, each time your opponent finishes one of his pieces and takes it off the board you must take another drink.

Variations for Party Animals:

Each time your opponent throws a double you must drink a full half of beer or one short, if it is a double six the penalty is itself double to a full pint or two shorts. Losing Party Animals have to pay the penalty of drinking a half of beer in one go or a short. If they are gammoned this is doubled up to a full pint or two shorts, backgammoned is a pint and a half or three shorts, and finally if you are so bad that you are bargammoned your penalty is a hefty two pints without stopping!

Drinking Drafts

Blitz Factor 5

A drinking game based on the board game of drafts. Ideally the playing pieces in this game should be replaced with small single shot or double shot glasses. If you do not have enough shot glasses use the normal playing pieces and keep a shot glass to the side constantly filled up with your preferred liquid.

How to Play:

Fill the shot glasses with your drinks. One of the players (who is taking the part of the black pieces) should add a touch of red food colouring or, if you prefer, Creme de Cassis. This will enable you to distinguish between the two different sets of pieces.

It is recommended that you use beer for this game, since so much drinking will take place that stronger drinks could have a severely detrimental effect on your brain.

Arrange the glasses as you would the normal pieces and commence playing according to the standard rules of drafts. Each time one of your pieces is taken you must drink the contents of the glass (if you are using standard pieces then you should empty the glass by the side of the board and immediately refill it). The losing player has to empty all of the glasses that remain on the board.

Variation for Party Animals:

Set a time limit for each move to take place of around 5 to 10 seconds. If there are more than two players, then play the standard game with the loser staying on for the next match.

Dominoes

Blitz Factor 2

An easy to play game requiring only a partner, a set of dominoes and some drinks.

How to Play:

Each time a player lays down a domino his opponent must take a drink. If he lays a double his opponent must take two drinks. If you have to take a domino from the pile to be able to play then you must take a drink.

Slugs & Ladders

Blitz Factor 4

You will be requiring a copy of the children's board game 'Snakes & Ladders', a large bladder, and a vindictive personality.

How to Play:

The game is played with no modifications to the boards, pieces or die. Simply throw the die and progress along the board as normal. However when you come to the base of a ladder you move your piece up the ladder and count the number of squares that the ladder passes through. This is the number of drinks that you can award to any of your opponents. Note it is not the number of squares that you have progressed, which could end up with somebody going to hospital. You can award the drinks to anybody but no more than three to any one person.

When you find yourself at the top of a snake you must move your piece down to its tail and, again, count the number of squares the snake goes through. That is the number of drinks you must take yourself and they must be drunk within the next four throws of the die.

The winner may award a bonus of 10 drinks to his opponents, this time with a limit of five per person.

Beeropoly

Blitz Factor 2

A boozy version of the favourite boardgame Monopoly. Players progress around the board as they would in the usual version, by throwing the dice, but payment for all properties, rents, fines, etc. are in beer.

How to Play:

The 'conversion rate' for game currency into drink must be set at the start of the game and really defines the actual Blitz Factor for the game. **Party Animals** wishing for a giant headache and a short game may choose to convert £100 of game money into a bottle of beer. Sane people, on the other hand, may plump for a sip instead..

Where payments are less than the set amount (in this case £100) the penalty is rounded up or down to the nearest unit. So a rental payment of £40 is scrubbed, whereas a purchase for £160 would equate to two units (bottles, sips or fingers). A gentler version overall allows board money to be interspersed with drinks - a player being able to choose which they use to pay with.

Payments to and from the bank are open to local rules. Some prefer to ignore payment from the bank to a player, and others will say that everyone else should take a drink. More house rules include ideas such as disallowing toilet breaks unless that particular player owns an utility and a visit to jail being paid for with a whisky.

Tactics:

The start of the game is by far the hardest when you need to purchase your properties. Depending on your viewpoint, this helps the evening of to a flyer, or it can lead to an early exit. You do, of course, have the option not to buy a certain location even if it is still available, but you could pay dearly later on. Imagine the state you could be in if you land on Mayfair with a hotel on it!

On the other hand, you may adopt the strategy that no-one will last long enough to erect such lucrative buildings. To avoid this initial Blitz Factor increment, try dealing the properties out between all the players.

Mad Man's Chess

Blitz Factor 5

A game of Chess where the different pieces each carry their own level of penalties. The frequency of drinking is not as high as in most games but when you do pay a penalty it is

fairly large. Grand masters are banned and speed Chess is not recommended.

How to Play:

For each player you will need 8 x 330ml cans and 8 x 440ml cans of your preferred beer, two of the larger cans should be of premium strength. Each players Pawns are represented with one of the 330ml cans whilst the pieces are represented by the 440ml cans, the King and Queen being the premium pieces. The cans should be split between the players and each keeps those representing his own pieces on his side of the board. The game is then played as normal and each time one of your pieces is captured you must drink the corresponding can. You may take as long as you like to consume a can unless another of your pieces is captured in which case you must down it immediately.

Other penalties come into force when pieces are castled, exchanged or when the King is put into check. Castling is generally considered to be a good move and when you castle your own pieces your opponent must drink from his King and also from his Rook. When you exchange one of your Pawns for another piece, usually a Queen, your opponent must drink a can related to that Pawn. And each time your King is put into check you must take a sip from your premium can. Although the game may take a long time you are not allowed to leave the table to visit the toilet. If you do, then you must forfeit one of your pieces and of course drink its equivalent can. Finally, the loser must not only drink his own King's can but also that of his opponent.

Card
Games

Blind Poker

Blitz Factor 3

A card game where you raise the stakes without knowing the value of your own card.

How to Play:

Deal one card to everybody in the room face down so that nobody can see them and place the remainder of the cards on the table also face down. Everybody then picks up their card, **without looking to see what it is**, and places it on their forehead face outwards.

The aim of the game is to land the person with the lowest value card (aces high) with the largest number of drinks. However, you won't know if YOU are going to be that loser.

The person to the left of the dealer opens the bidding with, say, one drink. The next person may raise to two or three drinks, etc. At any point, if someone suspects they have the lowest card, they can 'fold' and drink the highest bid for that round. The others keep on playing until play has returned to the dealer. Everyone then looks at their cards and the holder of lowest card drinks the final bid.

Bottle Blow

Blitz Factor 2

A simple game for people with wet lips.

How to Play:

Delicately balance a pack of cards on top of an empty bottle - this may take some doing if you have already played a couple of games. Players then take turns to blow some cards from the top of the pile onto the floor.

If any of the cards that fall to the floor reveal an Ace then that player must take a drink as a penalty. Should they reveal a Jack then they must take two drinks.

The player who blows the last card off the bottle must drink a full glass of beer.

Should any player fail to blow even a single card off the bottle on their turn then they must drink. Anyone who touches the bottle at any point of the game must also drink. And anybody who knocks the deck of cards off the bottle by any means other than blowing must drink a full glass of beer in one go.

Village Idiot

Blitz Factor 4

A card game for the ruling glasses.

How to Play:

This game requires at least five people to play. To start the game off everyone is dealt one card from the pack. The highest card becomes the King, the second highest the Queen, the lowest card is the Village Idiot and all the rest are the plebiscite.

Now everybody is dealt six different cards and each player is allowed to look at them. It is then the King who plays the first card and this can be anyone from his hand. The Queen goes second and that player must hold a card of higher value than the King over the top of it. If it can't go higher then they must of course take a drink. Play progresses round the table with the Village Idiot always being the last person to play. At any point in the game the King can demand that everybody else takes a drink. Similarly the Queen may command that everybody other than the King must drink. The Plebs are allowed to ask one another to drink and of course the Village Idiot but they are only allowed one such ruling per game. The Village Idiot is the bottom of all and he cannot ask anybody to drink, not even himself.

The game continues until all the cards have been used. The first player to finish becomes the King for the next game, the second person to finish becomes the Queen and the last person to finish becomes the next Village Idiot. Everybody should then change seats to reflect the new hierarchy with the Queen sitting to the left of the King and the Village Idiot to the right. It is also the Village Idiot's job to deal the cards, collect them in at the end and to refill everybody else's glasses.

Tactics:

Play your lowest cards first and always remember to abuse your power when you are the King or the Queen.

Variations:

If a player has a pair in his hand he may choose to play both cards at the same time. The player following must then play two higher cards. If the player can play two cards of a higher value then the one following him will just need to beat the highest of the two cards he has played, if he cannot play two higher cards then he must have two drinks and the onus moves onto the next player in line who must produce the two higher cards. Similarly, if somebody possesses three cards of the same value and it is their turn to start they may play all three in a similar manner to the two's. And finally, another twist for the Village Idiot is that he must give the King his highest card and the King may return his lowest card to the Village Idiot.

Some people like to play with the rules but the King can call a meeting of the Court. For such a meeting everybody must fill their glasses to the top and wait for the King to start drinking. When he does everybody must copy and drink at the same time and they are not allowed to stop drinking until somebody of higher rank than them stops before them. So the Queen can only stop drinking when the King has.

All the Nines

 Blitz Factor 2

A card game for the mathematically inclined.

How to Play:

Each person is dealt four cards which they are allowed to look at and then one card is turned over in the middle of the table. Play then progresses round the table in a clockwise direction with each person placing one card on the pile. You then have to keep track of the total score of the cards in the pile with Jacks, Kings and Queens scoring 10 and Aces scoring 11. When you play a card which brings a total in the pile to a number with 9 such as 19, 29 or 49, then you can request any other player to have a drink. It is up to each player to keep track of the pile score and if a dispute arises you can either choose to go for a recount or continue with the consensus of the group. Of course, if you have miscalculated the total and claim to give somebody a drink and are found subsequently to be wrong then you must take two drinks as penalty. The game stops when the pile score has reached 99 at which point everybody other than the player who played the last card must take a double drink.

If the total in the middle ever reaches the total 69 this is cause for special celebrations at which point everybody must have three drinks. After playing a card you take another from the stack left after the initial deal.

Pyramid

Blitz Factor 4

A geometrical card game with rapidly escalating penalties.

How to play:

Place five cards face down in a row on the table. Then create a new row with four cards, a third with three, then two and finally the fifth row with just one card. The remaining cards are then dealt out between the players ensuring everybody gets the same number of cards. Any remainders are left in a stack by the side of the table.

The first player then takes one card from the first row of the Pyramid (the one containing five cards). Keeping the card close to their chests they then announce to the rest of the players which card it is they have just picked up. They may either tell the truth or a complete lie. If somebody thinks that player is lying then immediately shout out "bullshit". The player must then reveal the card and if he is found to be bluffing he must drink **one** drink corresponding to the **first row** of the game. If, on the other hand, he has correctly described his card then the challenger must drink one drink. Should the player lie about the card he has just picked up and nobody challenges them, then they reveal the card and can choose any victim to have a drink.

Row 5 = 5 drinks

Row 4 = 4 drinks

Row 3 = 3 drinks

Row 2 = 2 drinks

Row 1 = 1 drink

Play continues around the group in a clockwise direction until the first row of the Pyramid has all been turned over. It is then time to move onto the second row of the Pyramid where all of the penalties become two drinks. Similarly on the third row penalties are three drinks, then four for the fourth row up to five drinks for the last card on the table.

Variation: To increase the Blitz Factor a wrong challenge of "Bullshit" automatically doubles the penalties for that row. So an incorrect challenge on row two would cause all subsequent penalties to become four drinks.

Killer

Blitz Factor 1

Also known as 'Wink Murder'

How to Play:

Remove one card from the pack for every player present **plus** the Ace of Spades. Place the remaining cards in the centre of the table, shuffle all the ones that you have removed including the Ace of Spades and deal one to each player. The card which is left over goes back into the pack on the top.

Everyone now looks at the card they have been dealt without telling anyone else which one they have got. The person with the Ace of Spades becomes an Assassin. They must set about killing everyone else at the table by winking at them. This is to be done surreptitiously because if they are spotted winking at somebody else then they have been exposed and they must down a full drink in one go without stopping. The person who spots the Assassin receives an exemption for the next game meaning that no matter what happens they will not have to drink. If on the other hand you get killed by a wink from the Assassin without anybody else spotting them doing so then you must die. This should be as dramatic as possible involving throwing yourself backwards, diving on the table, clutching your throat, etc but also you must have a drink. Any false accusations also result in a drink.

Note: It is possible for nobody to be the murderer (the ace having been returned to the pack). But that doesn't stop the accusations flying!

Straight Bullshit

Blitz Factor 3

A mentally challenging game for three to six people.

How to Play:

Everyone sits around a table and the deck of cards is dealt out as evenly as possible. The object of the game is to get rid of all of your cards.

The person to the left of the dealer is first to go and must place any number of cards of the same denomination as they like face down in the middle of the table. They must also announce to the table how many cards they have laid and of which denomination they are - they may lie or they may tell the truth. The next player must lay down as many cards as they like but the denomination must be one higher than the previous person to go. So, for example, if the first person lay three Jacks the second person must lay as many Queens as they possibly can.

If someone thinks or can work out from their own hand that you are lying they say "bullshit". If they are right the person laying the cards must take as many drinks as cards they claim to lay and they also pick up the cards from the centre of the table. If on the other hand the accusing player is wrong then they must drink as many cards as were laid and pick up the deck.

Play continues from low to high, returning back to two once the Aces have been passed. You may choose to stop once someone runs out of cards or continue down to the last two players who will be invited to drink a full glass each.

Ringer

Blitz Factor 4

A game requiring two packs of cards.

How to Play:

Everyone sits round the table after the two packs of cards have been shuffled together. The first person draws a card and shows it to the table. The next person draws a card and if it is related to the first card (meaning it has the same value or is a member of the same suit) then both players must drink a sip from their beer.

The third person now draws a card and shows it to the table. If it is related to either the first or the second card then all three players have to drink. Similarly if the third card drawn is related to the first second or third card then all four must count. The game continues until the ring is broken and a new game commences with the first card being drawn by the person following the one who broke the circle.

Variation: If any of the cards drawn matches a previous card exactly in suit and number then the owners of the two cards must take as many sips as the value of their card (Jacks =11, Queens = 12, Kings = 13).

Dictator

Blitz Factor Variable

Despots around the world will love this one.

How to Play:

All players draw one card to start the game, and the highest value indicates who will be dictator for the first game. The dictator then deals two cards to each player face down on the table in front of them.

When he has finished dealing he must dictate the conditions for the game and the penalties that will be given. For example, he may say that all red cards deserve one sip, that Kings deserve two sips, and that the Ace of Spades warrant a full glass to be downed in one. Players then turn their cards over and drink according to the rules.

Being a dictator, the dealer may also impose non-card based rules, such as penalties for scratching your nose, licking your lips or putting your elbows on the table.

Dealer

Blitz Factor 3

A game of Drug Dealers and Police for the modern party.

How to Play:

Take a card for every person at the party and in-cluded one King and one Ace. Then shuffle the cards and give everyone one card. The person with the King is the Policeman. The person with the Ace is the Drug Dealer. Everyone else are ordinary city folk going about their normal lives.

It is the Drug Dealers job to wink at any of the by-standers at the party. They must do this discretely and make sure they are not noticed by the Cop. When somebody has been winked at, noticing it can be difficult after a few games, they announce that a "deal has been made" to the rest of the party.

Once the deal has been announced the Policeman must set about deciding who is the Dealer. When they accuse somebody that person must reveal their card and if it is not the Ace the Policeman must drink the score on the card. The Policeman then chooses another and if wrong again must drink the number on that card as well. Play continues until the Policeman finally gets it right then the Drug Dealer must drink the number of spots on the Policeman's card.

Bottom Card

Blitz Factor 2

Ideal for post-meal drinks.

How to Play:

Each player is dealt a card which they may look at and then place face down in front of them on the table. One card is then placed face up in the middle of the table and the remaining deck placed next to them. The object of the game is not to end up with the lowest value card.

The player to the left of the dealer starts. They have three choices. They may stick with the card they already have, swap their card with the one which is already face up in the middle of the table, or swap their card with the top card of the unrevealed pile (their original card going on top of the revealed card in the middle). Play then progresses around the table with each player having one go. Once the last person has made their choice everybody reveals their card and the person with the lowest card must drink the number of spots on that card.

Variation: A simple variation with a higher Blitz Factor. In this game the object of the exercise is not to end up with the highest card. This simply increases the number of drinks that the loser must invite.

Quick Game

Geyser. Tap the bottom of your bottle firmly and squarely on the lip of a fellow drinkers bottle and stand back. Foam will erupt from the neck and cover the holder.

For Amusement Only

Asteroids

 *Blitz Factor 4*

For two people at any one time, but it is a quick game so play can progress around the room if more than two wish to play.

How to Play:

The Starship Commander deals six cards to the Space Pilot. These should be face down on the table in front of the Pilot and represent an asteroid belt. The Pilot then turns over the first card.

If that card is a non-face card then the Pilot has successfully negotiated that asteroid and nothing happens. If, however, it is a face card the Pilot is dealt an additional card for a Jack, two additional cards for a Queen and three for a King.

In addition they must take a drink for each card that they receive. The game continues until the Pilot has successfully negotiated the complete asteroid field.

High-Low

Blitz Factor 3

Similar to Asteroid but this time you see what you are up against.

How to Play:

The Controller deals out seven cards face up on the table. He then returns the first card and then prepares to turn another card over to place it on top of that card. The other player must now guess if the card he is about to turn over is higher or lower than the card already on the table. If he is correct, the card is laid on top of the original card and nothing else happens. If he is incorrect he must drink as many cards as he is from the end. So if you get it wrong on the first card you must drink seven drinks, while if you get it wrong you will only need to drink three.

Variation:

This carries a much higher Blitz Factor and could get as high as five. In this game when you get a card wrong, not only do you drink as many cards as you are from the end but you must return to the start!

Beggar your Neighbour

Blitz Factor 5

The closer you are the more you blow your neighbours away. A highly vindictive game and hence the high Blitz Factor.

How to Play:

A player is given one card from the pack. They must then guess whether the next card will be higher or lower. If correct they get to keep that card. If incorrect they must drink the number of cards that they have in their hand. Once they have guessed at least three correct cards then they may choose to "pass" or to continue.

Once they choose to pass, the cards are then handed over to the next player in line who continues to add to the pile by guessing correctly. The aim of the game is to build up as many cards as possible before passing it on to the next player, who gets thumped with a large number of drinks.

Note: If a card is equal to the previous card then this is counted as a loss.

Kings

Blitz Factor 3

A game for at least four people to be played in a bar with shorts instead of beer.

How to Play:

The cards are shuffled and dealt one at a time face up to each player. The first person to be dealt a King from the pack must choose a short. The second person to receive a King must pick a mixer, whilst the third will pay for the drink at the bar. The fourth person to receive a King from a pack must drink the concoction.

Tactics: You can have a good laugh devising a really evil mixture, but do not forget you could end paying for it and having to drink it.

Quick Game

Iron Head. Crush a can on your head. But before you do, make a small dent in the side and you'll discover remarkably little resistance.

For Amusement Only

Queens

Blitz Factor 3

A battle of the sexes.

How to Play:

The cards are shuffled and placed in the centre of the table. Anyone starts and picks a card from the top. If it is a Jack then all the men must drink, and if it is Queen then all the ladies must drink, a King and everyone must drink, an Ace and all members of the opposite sex must drink.

Variation for Party Animals:

As above, but when an 8 is turned over all players must provide some form of proof as to their gender. If it is acceptable or not should be decided by a vote from the entire group.

Jacks

Blitz Factor 3

It is all about volume.

How to Play:

Everyone starts with a full glass of beer and an empty jug is placed in the middle of the table. A pack of cards is shuffled and placed next to the jug. The first person must now pick a card from the pack If it is a red card he must take one sip from his glass and if it is a black card he must sip twice. If, on the other hand, it is a Jack then he may pour any amount of beer from his glass into the central jug. Play continues until the fourth

Jack is revealed and that player must drink the entire contents of the jug. However - and it is a big however - if you reveal a Jack and you have no more beer left in your glass to pour into the jug then the volume of the jug is doubled and he must attempt to drink it in one go.

Countdown

Blitz Factor 5

How cruel can you be?

How to Play:

All players are dealt one card face down in front of them on the table. Player one now turns over their card followed by player two. If the two cards belong to the same suit then player three tells players one and two to start drinking and he starts counting from one upwards. Only when player three has counted up to the number corresponding to their cards can players one or two stop.

For example should player one have played over the foour of diamonds and player two turned over the seven of diamonds then player one can stop when player three has counted to four and player two can only stop when he has counted to seven. It is entirely up to player three as to how quickly they count.

Player three now turns over their card. This is compared to player two's card and conditions for drinking apply. This time, if they match suit, it is player four's turn to count.

Bullshit Pyramids

Blitz Factor 4

A combination of those two great favourites "Bullshit" and "Pyramids".

How to Play:

Each player is given four cards face down in front of them and they may look at them but they should not show anybody else. The dealer then creates a pyramid with seven cards in row one, six in row two, five in row three, etc up to one in row seven. The first card of row one is now turned over to be exposed. If anybody has a card which

Drinking Games
Facts & Myths

Myth: Drinking Games can only be played with beer.

Myth: Only men play Drinking Games.

Fact: Drinking Games are played in enough countries to warrant inclusion in the Olympic Games.

Myth: *Turning Water into Wine* is the first recorded Drinking Game.

Fact: The presence of brain cells inhibits your ability to play Drinking Games.

Myth: Nobody has ever survived a game of Beer Hunter.

Fact: Nobody has ever survived a game of Beat the Barman.

Fact: Lager drinkers have small balls.

Myth: The author has small balls.

matches the one which has been turned over in number and colour then they can ask anybody else in the game to drink the number corresponding to the row. However since it is a "bullshitting" game, that person may either drink or challenge the person asking them to drink.

If they incorrectly challenge and the person asking them to drink does indeed have a card with the same colour and number as the upturned card, then they must drink double the row number. If, on the other hand, the challenge is successful and the person who has asked them to drink does not have a corresponding card then it is they who must drink double the row number.

Red and Black

Blitz Factor 3

Or should that be Black and Red.

How to Play:

A deck of cards is placed face down in the middle of the table. The first person predicts whether the top card is Red or Black, and then turns over the card. If correct they continue, if incorrect they drink. If they get three correct in a row then the game passes to the next person and the original player can create a rule which will stay in force till the end of the game. Some sample rules may include not being allowed to say the word "black", "holding your nose while you drink", or "standing on one leg while you turn over your card". Naturally any body caught breaking a rule must drink.

Mixers

Blitz Factor 4

A variation of Red and Black which require bitter and lager and uses two cards instead of one.

How to Play:

The first person must predict the colour of the top two cards in the deck. They have the choice of predicting red (for two red cards), black (two black cards), or purple (one red and one black card). If they are correct play moves onto the next player and the rule is created. But if they are wrong their penalty depends on "how wrong" they have been. An incorrectly predicted red results in a drink of lager whilst a black means a bitter. So, if you predict black and two reds are turned over you must drink two drinks of bitter, but if you predict purple and two reds are turned over you will only need to drink one bitter.

Chase the Ace

 Blitz Factor 2

Block your friends with a drink.

How to Play:

Aces rank high, and the object of the game is to not end up with the lowest card. Each player receives one card face down in front of them which they are allowed to look at. If anyone has an Ace then they turn this over immediately and they take no further part in this round of the game.

Next the player to the left of the dealer looks at his card and decides whether to swap with the person next to them or to stick. However, you cannot trade with the person who has an Ace and these act as blockers in the circuit. So, the person to the right of an Ace is in a difficult position because if they are given a low card they have nobody to trade with. Dealer, who goes last, has the choice of sticking or trading with the top card on the remaining pile. At the end of the round the person with the lowest card must drink. If there is a tie for the lowest card then all of them must drink.

Word Association

 ## *Blitz Factor 3*

A thinking drinking card game with words.

How to Play:

Take a pack of cards and then remove all of those below 10. Then place a full litre of beer in the middle of the table. Next arrange all 20 remaining cards in a circle around the jug.

The first player now takes any card from the circle and takes on one of five actions according to its face value:

An Ace - No action for the first three Aces but if it is a fourth Ace exposed then you must drink the remaining contents of the jug.

King - You must take a drink.

Queen - Give a drink to anyone of the other players.

Jack - A social, and everyone must drink.

10 - Word association.

With "Word Association" the first person to reveal a 10 can say any word they like. The next person to reveal a 10, however, must IMMEDIATELY give an associated word. If there is any pause then that player must drink and if there is no word association at all then they must drink twice. The worst penalty is to repeat a word that has already been said which is the same as revealing the fourth Ace and you must finish the jug.

Snap

 *Blitz Factor 5*

A quick moving, high drinking, low brain powered game as played by children.

How to Play:

The dealer, who is excluded from drinking in each round, holds a pack of cards and turns one card over and places it in the middle of the table. He then moves straight on and turns the second card over placing it on top of the first card.

Play continues like this until two cards with the same face value follow one another. This is a "snap", and the first person to shout "snap" and place their hand on top of the deck wins the top card.

They can then give as many drinks as there is on the card to any other player in the game (Jacks, Queens and Kings count as 10). The game ends when the dealer runs out of cards, and the person who has drunk the most in that round becomes the new dealer.

Variation:

If snap did not give enough chances for drinking some people included new conditions for a "snap" to ensure a rapid end to the evening. These conditions could be two cards with the same suit, two face cards, or two cards in ascending order.

Quick Game

Wet Foot. Drain a beer bottle and fill it with water to within 2cm of the mouth. Now strike the top of the bottle with the palm of your hand. The lower half of the bottle will erupt in a shower of glass and water.

For Amusement Only

Spoons

Blitz Factor 3

Apart from beer, cards, and mad people, you will be needing a quantity of spoons equal to one less than the number of players.

How to Play:

All the spoons are placed in the centre of the table and a pint of beer is prepared and placed at another location for reasons which will become apparent. The dealer then gives four cards to each player including himself and places the remaining deck upside down in front of them. Everyone looks at their cards and the dealer takes a top card from the pack. He must now decide which of his five cards he is going to discard and give to a person on his left.

The person on the left now follows suit, deciding whether to keep the card he has been given or to pass it onto a person on their left. When play reaches the last person in the circle their discarded card forms a new pile in front of the dealer. It continues until all cards in the original pile have been used at which point the dealer shuffles the discarded pile and starts again.

If any person in the game creates a hand with four of a kind or a straight they quickly grab a spoon from the middle of the table. This is a signal for everyone else to grab which they do as quickly as possible. The person left without a spoon at the end must drink the beer. It is the physical nature of this game, the drunken lunges which take place, which suggests that the beer should be kept on a separate table.

Suck Me

Blitz Factor 1

A game about breaking down social barriers and getting drunk. It suggested that you play with an equal number of males and females, but that is up to you!

How to Play:

Everyone sits in a circle and most people prefer to alternate male and female. The first person then chooses and picks a card from the top of the pack and holds it against their lips just by sucking air quickly through their mouth. They must then pass that card to the person to their left who receives the card by sucking equally as hard. They, in turn, must pass the card to the person on their left. Again using suction power only. If the card is dropped in any exchange then both players must drink the number on the card.

Variation for Party Animals:

Carries an even lower Blitz Factor but can be more fun. If a card is dropped any exchange apart from just drinking the card is ripped in two. One half of the card is now thrown away and the second half of the card must progress in the same manner as the original game. Before long and after a few beers the card will be down to a quarter or an eighth of its original size. Lips will become significantly larger than the remaining piece of card.

Beer Jack

Blitz Factor 2

Black Jack without the money.

How to Play:

Each person is dealt two cards, one face up one face down. The player to the left of the dealer now looks at his hand without revealing it to the others and decides whether to take one card from the dealer or to stick. The object is to get as close to 21 as possible with face cards counting as 10 and Aces counting as 11. When the third card has been revealed they choose yet another card or again choose to stick.

Once they have chosen to "stick" play progresses to the next person round the table on the left. The banker is the last person to play and may reveal all of their cards to the table. The game ends when the banker has taken as many cards as they need from the pack and chosen to stick. Drinks are now awarded according to scores:

● Anyone scoring less than the banker takes as many drinks as the banker has cards.
● The banker taking as many drinks as there are people in the game who beat him.

At the end of each round the banker and dealer should pass to the person to the right of the original dealer.

Jail Break

Blitz Factor 3

The actual Blitz Factor depends on your ability to get out of jail quickly.

How to Play:

The cards are dealt out face down to each player who is allowed to look at them but should not show them to anybody else. The person to the left of the dealer now plays any card. The next person round must play a card of the same face value otherwise they "go to jail" and must take a drink. The person to left of the dealer now plays any card and the direction of play is changed meaning that the person "in jail" must play a card of the same value. If they do play a card then they are out of jail and free to go, otherwise they must take another drink.

Play continues until any one player has played their last card. At the end of the game everybody must take as many drinks as they have cards in their hands.

Up and Down the River

 *Blitz Factor 5*

Requires one full deck of cards for every five people playing.

How to Play:

Deal four cards face up in front of each player and designate one person (the dealer) as the rower of the boat. The rower now strokes his way up the river by turning over one card from the deck. Anyone who has a card in front of them matching the number on the rower's card (ignoring suit) must drink one drink. The rower now continues up river and takes his second stroke by turning over another card. This time anyone matching the card revealed by the rower must take two drinks. The rower continues up the river until they have taken their fourth stroke or fourth card, with players taking penalties as necessary.

When everyone has completed taking their four drinks the oarsman now turns around his boat and rows back down the river by revealing another card. This time, if anybody matches the card revealed they have four drinks **to give away**. They may choose to give four drinks to one person, one drink to four people, or any possible combination. The next card revealed gives anyone matching it the right to give away three drinks, etc until the boat is back at the jetty. The game continues until every player has had a go at rowing the boat.

The rower turns over	Anyone matching drinks
first card	one drink
second card	two drinks
third card	three drinks
fourth card	four drinks

The rower now turns around,

The rower turns over	Anyone matching
fifth card	gives away four drinks.
sixth card	" " three "
seventh card	" " two "
eighth card	" " one "

Coin
Games

Rounders

Blitz Factor 2

Requires four shot glasses and a jug of beer.

How to Play:

Place all four shot glasses in a row and fill them with beer. Then split the players into two teams, home and away.

The away team starts and their first player steps forward with a 1p piece. Their aim is to bounce the 1p coin off the table and into one of the shot glasses, then they must drink the beer from the shot glasses behind the one in which it lands. For example if it lands in the third glass then they only have one drink, however if it lands in the first glass then they must drink the remaining three. Failure to hit any of the bases results in you having to drink all four glasses.

After drinking, the glasses are refilled and that player's coin is placed by the side of the glass it landed in. The second player now comes forward and takes his turn to bounce the coin into the glass. And as with the normal game of rounders the previous players coin moves forward to stay one glass or one base in front of the following player. When the coin reaches the end that counts as a run and you score for that team.

Missing all four glasses also results in being caught and your coin is removed from the game. Three catches and the batting team are all out. The game ends when both teams have had two innings. Add up the teams scores and the losing team must pay for the beer.

Pennies - 1

Blitz Factor 3

This game acts as a basis for most of the coin games.

How to Play:

Obtain a shallow whiskey glass and place it in the middle of the table. All the players stand around the table with a 1p coin in their hand. Then they take turns trying to bounce their coin off the table and into the glass. If you are successful you can tell any other player to have a drink and you receive a second go. If you fail then you forfeit your go and the next person in the circle takes their turn. However, if you are good enough to get three bounces into the glass in a row you can create a rule for the game. This could be anything such as "allowed to say yes or no", you must stand on one leg, or use your left hand to bounce the coin. Actually if anybody breaks one of the rules during the game you must drink.

Pennies - 2

The glass is filled with beer. The successful player can ask anybody to drink that glass with the coin still in it (obviously trying not to swallow it).

Pennies - 3

If the player bounces the coin and hits the rim of the glass without it going in. They must drink the glass themselves.

Pennies - 4

Double or Quits. If a player bounces and misses instead of the play progressing to the next player they can announce "Double or Quits". They take another turn and if successful they can ask somebody to drink two drinks or they must drink two themselves. It is wise to set a limit of three double or quits for any one player.

Did you say, "drink"?

If so, then you should...

- Quaff
- Swig
- Curl a Can
- Get it down
- Drain the vessel
- Exercise the elbow
- Toss it back
- Guzzle
- Imbibe
- Partake of the fluid
- Polish it off
- Eat froth
- Gulp
- Hoist one
- Slam it

Pennies - 5

Having made three successful bounces and created a new rule for the game you may wish to continue and attempt for five success known as a "kill". A successful kill allows you to ask somebody to drink a full bottle of beer without stopping, but a failure means that you must do the same.

Ice Cube Pennies

 *Blitz Factor 4*

In addition to some pennies you will need a standard ice cube tray.

How to Play:

Players bounce a coin off the table and into the ice cube tray. If the coin lands on the left side of the tray then the bouncer must take a drink but if it lands on the right hand side of the tray they can give a drink to any of the other players. The number of drinks is dictated by how many rows back the coin lands in the ice tray. One player continues until they either miss the tray or they hit the take side and need a drink themselves.

Speed Pennies

Blitz Factor 4

This game keeps everything moving faster and does not allow those boring farts that stay sober and concentrate on playing properly.

How to Play:

Quite simply this a game of pennies but one on one. Two players stand at opposite sides of the table and try to bounce their pennies into the same glass, with the loser drinking the beer with the penny in it (obviously trying to avoid swallowing the penny).

Quick Game

Two-in-One. While drinking from one glass, use your other hand to fill it from a second glass. Sounds simple but is sure to impress.

For Amusement Only

Taps

Blitz Factor 2

The perfect game for people who are too drunk to talk.

How to Play:

Everyone sits around the table with the coin in their hand. The first person taps his coin on the table once for play to go right and twice for it to go to his left. If it was one tap then the person to his right must tap his coin either once or twice, and if it was two taps then the person on his left must tap their coin once or twice. When someone taps out of turn or does not tap enough then they must drink.

Spinners

Blitz Factor 1

A coin game verging on skill and endurance.

How to Play:

A group of people sit around a table with a one pence piece. The first person takes the penny and spins it on its edge and then calls the name of somebody else at the table. They must now flick the coin with their index finger to keep it spinning but not allow it to spin off the table. Once flicked they then call out the name of yet another person at the table. Anybody causing the coin to spin off the table must drink and anybody who allows the coin to stop spinning before they have flicked it must also drink. The person who last flicks the coin restarts following a failure.

Variation:

If the coin goes off the table that is equal to one drink. Landing head side up is equal to two drinks, and tail side up is equal to three drinks.

Chandeliers

Blitz Factor 3

How to Play:

Place a full pint of beer in the middle of the table and as many smaller glasses of beer as there are players in the circle around the central pint. Taking it in turns a player now tries to bounce their penny into someone's glass. If they succeed the player whose glass it is must drink that beer, otherwise the coin moves to the next player. If, on the other hand, the player gets their penny into the central pint then everybody except the coin bouncer must drink their drink as quickly as possible with the last to finish having to down the big pint in the middle.

Threshold

Blitz Factor 4

A game requiring a coin and a die with very little skill and definitely a high alcohol threshold.

How to Play:

Place a coin and a die in an empty glass. One person now shakes the glass and places it upside down in front of the person to their left. That person must now guess if the coin is going to show heads or tails. If they are correct then the shaker must drink as many spots as are showing on the die. If they are wrong then they must drink that many times.

Variation:

To increase the Blitz Factor to number 5, simply use two dice.

Dice
Games

Dice

Blitz Factor 5

Make sure you do not have any appointments for the next day.

How to Play:

Roll two dice and drink the following:

● Anything that adds up to 6 (2 and 4, 1 and 5) or contains a 6 in it (6 and 1, 6 and 2, etc) drink once.

● For a double 2, 4, or 5 you drink that many (2, 4 or 5) drinks.

● If you roll double 3 you are penalised twice for getting a double which adds up to 6 so take 4 drinks.

● Throwing a double 1 or double 6 is the worst, and you should drink a shot of whiskey or another short.

Keep on rolling until you get a combination not included in any of the above (and there are only nine of those).

Twenty One Eyes

Blitz Factor 2

Can be played with any number of dice.

How to Play:

Everyone sits around the table and takes a turn throwing a die. Keep a track of the number of eyes (one's) that are thrown. The person who throws the 7th eye chooses a drink from the bar, and the one who throws the 14th eye must pay for it.

Now each time an eye is thrown one die is taken from the game until only one remains so that the progression towards 21 is much slower. The person who throws the 21st eye must drink the chosen poison.

Beer Die

Blitz Factor 3

Requires a long table, strong glasses, and a steady aim.

How to Play:

Players face one another from opposite ends of a long table each with a full glass of beer in front of them. One team starts and throws a die in the air and aims to land it in the beer of the opposing team. If the die goes straight in one of their glasses the entire opposing team must drink their beers in one go. However, if the die just glances to the side of an opponent's glass they only need drink half of a beer.

The receiving team may seek to prevent the die from landing in their glasses by trying to catch it.

However they can only use one hand and the die must not touch any other part of their body. A clean catch results in a half drink for the throwing team, but a foul catch results in a full down in one. Finally, unless you are in possession of good head and eye protection, it is suggested that only under arm throws are allowed.

Variation: Place a row of shorts across the centre of the table to act as a net. Any die hitting the net results in a short for the last person to have touched the die.

Sixes

Blitz Factor 3

Can be played alone (for the sad git) or in a party.

How to Play:

Line up six half pint glasses in a row and number them from 1 to 6. Now throw a die and locate the glass corresponding to the number shown on the top. If the glass contains some beer then you must drink its contents, but if it is empty you may fill it with as much beer as you wish. After filling a glass the die moves on to the next person.

Man 'O Three Tails

Blitz Factor 5

A fairly complex scoring game so you will probably need to keep a table of penalties in front of you particularly after a few rounds.

How to Play:

Everyone roles one die and the first person to role a 3 becomes the Man 'O Three Tails. Now the person to the left of Man 'O Three Tails goes first and throws both dice taking the following actions:

1:1   Double, take two drinks
1:2   Adds up to 3 so the Man 'O Three Tails drinks
1:3   Contains the number 3 so the Man 'O Three Tails drinks
1:4   Put your thumb on the floor and keep it there until your next go is completed
1:5   Index finger on the side of your nose
1:6   Player to the left of the roller drinks
2:2   Two drinks
2:3   Man 'O Three Tails drinks
2:4   Free go

Drinking Games 2000

2:5   Player to the left of the roller takes one drink
2:6   Free go
3:3   You become the new Man 'O Three Tails
3:4   Man 'O Three Tails drinks
3:5   Man 'O Three Tails drinks
3:6   Man 'O Three Tails drinks
4:4   Two drinks
4:5   Social everybody drinks
4:6   Free go
5:5   Two drinks
5:6   Player to the right of the roller drinks
6:6   Man 'O Three Tails drinks four

Bullshit Dice

Blitz Factor 3

Standard Bullshit game but this time with dice.

How to Play: Take two dice and an opaque glass (that is one you cannot see through for the uneducated) and several people. Everyone sits round the table and one person arbitrarily starts. They shake both dice in the cup and turn it over in front of them onto the table. Now the shaker takes a peak at the two dice and announces to the other players the total score on the dice. As with all bullshit games this may be the truth or a lie.

The dice and cup are now handed to the next player who repeats the exercise by shaking the dice and upturning the cup in front of them. This play HAS to exceed the score of a previous player either by getting a better throw or by bullshitting. Anyone around the table can challenge any throw at any time. If a bullshit score is successfully discovered then the thrower must drink, whilst an unsuccessful challenge results in a drink for the challenger. Should the real score on the dice ever equal a double during a challenge then the penalties are also doubled. Finally, the person following on from a double 6 (real only) must down a full beer in one go whether or not they place a challenge.

Speed
Games

Three Legged Pub Crawl

Blitz Factor 3

One of the oldest games in the book.

How to Play:

Very simple. Split into teams of two and tie one of your legs together. Then everyone starts in the same bar and each member of the team must consume a full beer. Once they have finished they must head as quickly as possible to the next watering hole where they consume another beer.

The first team to finish their beers at the last pub wins. The actual Blitz Factor is dependent on how many bars is visited but five is a good number. Toilet stops are allowed but the team must stay tied together.

Shot Gun

Blitz Factor 2

Be careful you do not cut your tongue.

How to Play:

Take a can of beer and put a small hole on the bottom of the can on the side using a screw driver or small punch. Now place the hole over your mouth and as you lift your head backwards as if to pour the beer down your throat open the can - and drink as fast as possible. The first person to finish is the winner.

Note: The Blitz Factor increases rapidly if more than one game is played.

Down Down

Blitz Factor 2

The most basic of all.

How to Play:

All players start drinking a full glass or tankard of beer at the same time. The first person to finish indicates they have done so by holding it upside down on top of their head. Anyone with beer left in their glass after the first person has finished must pour it over their heads.

Spirits is to be frowned upon as is inverting your glass above your head and claiming a win if you have not finished the contents. The penalty is another beer until they get it right.

Boat Race

Blitz Factor 2

Another classic.

How to Play:

Divide everyone into two teams who stand with a full glass of beer one behind the other. On the signal to "go" the first person at the front of the queue drinks their beer as quickly as possible.

As with "Down Down", they signal that they have finished their drink by inverting the empty glass on top of their heads. This is a sign for the second person in the team to start who then follows suit. The team to finish first are the winners - obviously !

Variation:

Each player has two glasses of beer. The race goes down the line as for a normal boat race but when it reaches the end the back drinker must drink both his beers and then the process is reversed back to the front of the line.

Endurance Games

Century Club

Blitz Factor 5

It sounds simple, but it ain't!

How to Play:

You will need a liquid measuring jug from a kitchen or pre-marked glasses, and a stop watch. It may also be worthwhile finding a tee-total time keeper.

Every minute, for 100 minutes, you must drink 30 millilitres (1 fl oz) of beer, no more, no less. At the start of the game you will be gasping for another drink but by the end you will be wondering and struggling, where the time is going.

Variation for Party Animals:

Assign a King and a Village Idiot to the group. No one except the King is allowed to go to the toilet. While the Village Idiot must drink double the quantity as the rest of the group, that is 60 millilitres at each minute interval. When the King goes to the toilet, they are immediately demoted to the Village Idiot upon their return. Also, the volume missed by their visit must be made up within the next two minutes. Anyone else going to the toilet, for the sake of public decency, must drink a penalty of 330 mls (that is a full can) in addition to the volume they missed.

Keg Stand

 *Blitz Factor 5*

Another game for the morally insane.

How to Play:

Perform a handstand in front of the keg and get a couple of friends to hold your legs. Now wrap your lips around the tap and get a third person to open it - start drinking.

The object of the game is to drink as much as you can for as long as you can but do not forget to have a signal for when you want to give up and have somebody close the tap. Compare your times and the person who kept drinking for the longest is the winner. They get a free pint.

Sixty Seconds

Blitz Factor 5

Requires a clock with a second hand.

How to Play:

Each person chooses a number from one to 60 which corresponds to a second in the minute. When the second hand of the clock passes the first number chosen that person must start drinking their pint and finish it within 60 seconds. When the second hand has returned to the number for the first player (that is when the 60 seconds for their drink is up) then the clock starts counting again from that point until the second chosen number is reached at which point the person with the second number starts drinking.

For example:

Player one chooses the number five, player two chooses the number 12, player three chooses the number 26, etc. The clock starts and counts round 1, 2, 3, 4, 5. at this point player one starts drinking and they have 60 seconds to complete that task. The second hand meanwhile does a full rotation of the clock and comes back to the number 5 and the game starts again. Now when it passes the number 12 the second player starts to drink and they also have 60 seconds to complete the task. Similarly when the hand has done a full rotation and come back to the number 12 the game starts again and the third person starts when it reaches 26.

Either play an open ended game which only finishes when somebody loses consciousness, or set a time limit such as one hour or two hours.

Seven Dwarfs

Blitz Factor 5

Play this only at parties or you'll lose friends at your local.

How to Play:

At any point during the evening any one of the participants can shout out "Hi Ho". This is a signal for everybody to finish the drinks they have in front of them as fast as possible. The first person to finish then becomes the only person who can shout "Hi Ho" for the next round. This can be at any point in the evening.

The seventh round is the important one (corresponding to a number of Dwarfs). The last person to finish their drink when the seventh "Hi Ho" has been announced must pay for the entire evening.

Beat the Barman

 *Blitz Factor 5+*

The most insane game in this book. Nobody has ever won, lost or drawn this game.

How to Play:

The drinker goes to the bar and orders a shot of anything. He then pays for the drink with too much money (in other words using a £5 note for a £2 drink). When the Barman goes back to the till to get the change the drinker downs the shot in one. When the Barman returns with your change return to the first step and ask for another shot.

The game ends in one of four ways:

1. The drinker falls over - the bar wins.
2. The Barman punches the drinker - draw.
3. The drinker gets thrown out onto the street - draw.
4. The bar closes - drinker wins, much celebration.

Tactics: Make sure the bar staff are friendly and can take a joke or a draw is on the cards. Also, don't play this game in a crowded bar or somebody else may pinch your barman.

We would very much like to hear from anybody who has played this game and lived.

TV and Film Related Games

Hoist One

S.M.A.S.H.

 Blitz Factor 3

Drinking to the drinking cult series M.A.S.H.

How to Play:

Watch any episode of the show and when the rank of Private is said take a drink. If anyone says Corporal take two drinks and Major warrants three.

Reservoir Dogs

 *Blitz Factor 5*

You will need a copy of the video Reservoir Dogs, but do not play if you have a weak stomach.

How to Play:

Quite simple - every time somebody says the word "Fuck" you drink. Nobody has ever made it to the end of the movie.

If you do, please let us know.

Rudolph

Blitz Factor 1

Ideal for the festive season.

How to Play:

Watch the Christmas classic Rudolph the Red Nosed Reindeer and every time his nose lights up take a drink. If his nose stays lit for a long time you continue drinking until it leaves the screen.

Bat Beer

Blitz Factor 3

Holy Cow! To be played watching any Batman film or TV show.

How to Play:

Every time somebody says Bat something you take a drink and when Robin says Holly something you must finish your drink completely. Be careful when the dangerous duo are in the Bat cave because you have to down a shot for every item with a Bat label on it.

TV Characters

Blitz Factor Variable

An adaptable game to be played with any TV programme.

How to Play:

Get hold of a copy of the TV listings and choose characters from a forthcoming programme. Between yourselves choose which characters you are going to represent and every time one of them appears you must drink until they leave the screen. If somebody is mentioned by name but does not appear then just take one short drink. This is ideal for soap programmes.

Simpsons

 ## *Blitz Factor 3*

You will catch this one on Satellite.

How to Play:

Take one drink every time:

- Homer eats a doughnut
- Lisa mentions humanity
- Bart makes a crank phone call
- Grandpa complains
- Marj growls at Homer
- Marj's sisters appear
- Flanders mentions God
- Itchy and Scratchy appear
- . Maggie falls down

Shaken Not Stirred

Blitz Factor 3

Any 007 will do.

How to Play:

Put on a James Bond film and every time someone says "James" drink twice and if they say "Bond" drink four times. Should the full name "James Bond" come out then you must drink a full beer. Therefore, when the man himself mutters the words "My names is Bond, James Bond" you need to down your own beer and take four other drinks.

Blues Brothers

Blitz Factor 4

Your mission is to drink.

How to Play:

Ask everyone to sign in and unless they place an "X" on the sheet they must start the evening with a full beer for being a virgin. Throughout the movie every time a car is wrecked you must drink half a beer until the last few minutes when a sip will do. Whenever the phrase "mission from God" is used you must down a full bottle.

Star Trek

Blitz Factor 3

Take it away Scottie.

How to Play:

Take a drink every time you hear the following:

- Captain's log
- Medical emergency
- Warp factor
- Belay that order
- Alien fleet
- Energise

Drinking Games 2000

- Beam
- Lithium crystals
- Federation
- Logical

- Any swear word
- Stun
- Peace
- Force field

Miscellaneous Games

Darts

Blitz Factor 2

Another variety of the standard game.

How to Play:

Taking three goes at a time, try and hit the bull. The first person to score a bulls eye names a drink, the second chooses who should pays for it, and the third chooses who should drink it.

Variation: Once

the drink has been chosen and before a purchaser has been decided upon anyone can hit a double and "double" the chosen drink. Similarly a dart in the inner ring trebles the drink.

Peanut Races

Blitz Factor 3

Needs a bag of shelled peanuts, preferably salted.

How to Play:

Each player has a full pint of lager and is given a peanut. On the count "3, 2, 1, go" the peanut is dropped into the glass and sinks to the bottom. The bubbles will form around the peanut and cause it to rise to the surface. The player whose peanut is last to come to the top must drink their full pint in one go complete with peanut and then go and buy another drink.

Anyone dropping their peanut too early, or missing their glass altogether is the loser of that round and must drink. Anyone pointing a finger at a loser of any particular round must join the loser in drinking their full pint.

Players must retrieve their peanuts at the end of each round and eat it before choosing a new one. The nuts should be laid out on a table in front of all players for choosing with the loser of the previous round getting first choice, the second last to finish getting second choice, etc.

Beer Pong

Blitz Factor 2

You need two tables and Ping Pong ball.

How to Play:

Place a large glass of beer on one table and the other table about six feet away. Players now take turns bouncing the Ping Pong ball off the near table and trying to land it in the glass on the far table. If the ball goes straight in the glass then all the other players must drink theirs down in one. If it should just glance the glass on the far table then the others need only take a sip from their drinks. On the other hand, if the player misses the far table all together they should down their drink in one. Missing the near table altogether is a heinous crime and you should drink the beer with the ball in it (taking care not to swallow it).

Beer Bungee

Blitz Factor 1

Good game for barbecues or open air entertainment.

How to Play:

Attach a bungee rope to a wall or a heavy table (with people sitting on it). And attach the other end to a willing participant preferably round the waist or an ankle (the neck is not recommended). Now place a smaller table approximately 1 1/2 times the length of the bungee away from the wall or large table. Then place a pint of beer or other drink on the small table. Quite simply it is the participant's task to drink the drink.

Drinking Games 2000

Radio Phone-Ins

 Blitz Factor 1

A game to play on your own.

How to Play:

Tune in to any radio phone in programme. Every time somebody says hello followed by the Host's name take a drink. If they announce that they are a "first time caller" down a full beer or a couple of shots. If anybody gets angry drink to them, and if they get cut off finish your drink to commiserate with them.

Variation:

To play with others in the room. Follow the same rules as above, but take turns dialing into the show yourselves. Anybody who gets anything other than an engaged signal must drink a full glass and anyone actually getting onto the show must drink two full drinks.

However, if you do get onto the show and manage to say hello to your friends everyone that you managed to mention before being cut off has to drink five.

Smile

Blitz Factor 1

How to Play:

Everyone sits around the table with a drink in front of them and the loser of the previous round now goes underneath the table to do whatever they like. No one is allowed to look under the table and must stare at the person opposite them. The first person to smile is the loser and must drink their chosen brew in one.

Variation for Party Animals:

Place a large tablecloth over the table which dangles down over people's thighs. At the start of a new game everyone drops their trousers or raises their skirts before anyone disappears under the table.

Matchbox

Blitz Factor 2

Can also be played with cigarette boxes.

How to Play:

Everyone sits around a table with their drink 2/5ths in front of them. The first player now throws a matchbox over their drink towards the middle of their table. If it lands flat they must drink 1/2 pint or one shot. If it lands on a long the edge 1/2 pint or one shot goes into the "kitty". And if it lands on a short edge then a full pint or two shots are added to the "kitty". Play now moves onto the next person who throws the matchbox in the same manner. From now on anybody landing the box on the flat edge must drink the "kitty".

Sink the Battleship

Blitz Factor 2
Sometimes called Depth Charge.

How to Play:

Take a pint glass or a large jug and float a short glass on top of the beer. Now each player takes turns pouring some beer into the short glass usually from a bottle. Wait at least 5-10 seconds before the next player takes a turn. The person who causes the glass to sink must drink the entire contents.

Quick Game

Whirlpool. If you fancy a quick race while drinking from a bottle, use a technique developed for draining a yard. Slowly turn the bottle as you drink and the fluid will swirl out rapidly rather than glugging in a stop/start manner.

For Amusement Only

Cigars

Blitz Factor 3

Only for smokers

How to Play:

The group buys a cigar and lights it. One person now takes a drag and passes onto the next player. Anyone who causes some ash to fall from the cigar must pay a penalty of an entire drink.

Beer Hunter

Blitz Factor 2

Russian roulette at its best.

How to Play

Take a six pack and shake one of the cans really hard. Now all but one player turns their back on the 6 pack and the cans are shuffled around. The shuffler now turns his back on the cans and another person takes a turn to shuffle them around. Once everyone has had a go at shuffling and nobody knows which is the can that was shaken each player picks up a can and holds it to their forehead. Now you take turns to open the can whilst keeping it pressed against your temple. If the can just opens then you must drink it, but if you get covered in beer the game starts again and you must buy the new six pack.

Lids

Blitz Factor 2

Played with lids from beer bottles.

How to Play:

Everyone kneels on the floor with a glass in front of them half filled with beer. One person starts and attempts to throw a beer bottle lid into somebody else's glass. If it lands in their glass and stays there that person becomes "live". The Live person now has a chance to redeem themselves by throwing the lid back into the glass of the person who just scored as hit on them. If they succeed then the hits are canceled out, but if they fail they must drink their drink.

It should be obvious who a player is aiming at when they throw their lid and they become the next person to throw. However if they are so drunk you do not know where it has been thrown towards, then the person closest to the lid takes the next turn.

Note: Use water in the glass if playing this at home and you do not want a beer on your carpets (but have the penalty beers handy).

Variation: Instead of a glass full of beer in front of you use a bottle of beer with the lid taken off and placed back on upside down. Your mission is now to knock a lid off somebody else's bottle with a spare lid.

Beer Pot

Blitz Factor 4

Timing is everything.

How to Play:

Everyone buys a drink and puts it in the pot. Now one person starts and drinks as much from the pot as they like. When they stop then the pot passes the next person who does the same thing. The pot passes around the group until one person empties the last glass and they are designated the winner. It is the person who drank immediately before the winner who is the loser and they should then pay for the new pot with one drink for each player.

Variation:

If finances are tight then the loser puts in two drinks instead of the whole lot, and the winner goes free, with everyone else putting in one.

AGM

 *Blitz Factor 4*

A good way to lose your job.

How to Play:

At your Annual General Meeting or any other occasion when your bosses get up to make those long boring speeches take a drink when any speaker uses these words:

- Hard Work
- Vision
- Future
- Management
- Shareholders
- Expansion
- Relations
- Budget
- Targets
- Incentives
- Profits

- Job
- Team
- Quality
- Down Sizing
- Dividends
- Management
- Sacrifice
- Scenario
- Opportunities
- Sales
- Net

And take three drinks when anyone says:

- Redundancies
- Pay Freeze
- Bonuses

- Voluntary
- Share Options
- Executive

Drinking Games 2000

Down a full one if anybody mentions:

- Awards the Company has received
- The environment
- The performance in relation to competitors
- The economic climate
- Change of Government

Slam two whenever a member of the Board congratulates another.

When anyone makes a joke, no matter how bad, start drinking and **don't stop** until the laughter has completely subsided.

If in doubt drink, for tomorrow you will be gone.

Beer Mats

Blitz Factor 1

Can be played in any pub.

How to Play:

Take a beer mat and rip off less than half of the mat and discard it. Now pass the mat to the next player who must also remove less than half. The person who can no longer tear any off the mat is deemed the loser and must buy the next round. In the absence of microscopes, group opinion will rule as to how much is acceptable as a minimum tear. Remember you can only remove less than half of the remaining mat and throwing away the largest section makes you the loser.

Matchsticks

Blitz Factor 2

Use one box of matches for every two players.

How to Play:

Create a pile of matchsticks in the middle of the table. Everyone takes turns picking up single matchsticks. However when you are picking up your matchstick you must not cause any other match to move at all. If you do, you lose, and must drink!

What did you shay?

Thumper

 ## *Blitz Factor 3*

Requires good co-ordination.

How to Play:

Each player chooses a sign to make such as waving their hand, giving a peace sign, nodding their head, stoking their stomach, picking their nose, etc. Everyone now sits in a circle and slaps their hands on their knees twice and then claps twice and continues to do so throughout the entire game. This should create a rhythm for the evening.

To start the action one player now asks "what's the name of the game". All the other players must yell "Thumper". The original player now responds "how do you play" and the rest reply "signs". The player who started this round now gives his sign during the thumping beats on their knees and a sign of another player during the clapping beats.

The player whose sign was shown during the clapping beat must now show their sign during the thumping beats and another sign during the clapping. This goes on until somebody makes a mistake; breaking the rhythm, forgetting their sign or mistaking somebody else's sign. The person who made the mistake must finish their drink and refill their glass before the game starts again with them asking "what is the name of the game".

Who Shit?

Blitz Factor 3

There's an awful lot of it about!

How to Play:

Everyone picks a name of an animals excrement - dog shit, cow shit, sheep shit, elephant shit, etc.

The game begins with someone shouting "someone shit on the floor". All the other players shout back "Who Shit?". The original player now picks someone's name, for example "Elephant Shit". The player who was named must now defiantly respond "Bull Shit!" to which the original player responds "Who Shit?". Now Elephant Shit blames somebody else who replies with "Bull Shit". As with Thumper, anyone who messes up must drink and then start the next round.

Fizz Buzz

Blitz Factor 3

One of the original word games.

How to Play:

Everyone sits around the table and you start counting from one upwards. The first player says, "one", the second says, "two", etc. However, any number that contains the number three or is divisible by three (for example 3, 23 and 12) must say, "fizz". Any which contains the number five or is divisible by five must say, "buzz".

Simple so far. However you must take note of the permutations of threes and fives. So 33 will be "fizz, fizz" and 55 will become "buzz, buzz". Likewise, the number 15 is divisible by three and five so it is pronounced "fizz, buzz".

Some players like to note the order in which the threes and fives arise. So 35 would be "fizz, buzz" while 53 would be "buzz, fizz". And the appearance of the number takes precedence over a factor. Thus 15 would be "buzz, fizz" since the number five occurs in the original, whilst three is a factor. However, policing such complexities becomes almost impossible the further the game goes and the more that is drunk.

Not Me

Blitz Factor 1

A simple game to play with a group of people that you know very well, but beware of playing it if your partner is present.

How to Play:

Everyone sits in a circle with their drink in hand. The host or person organising the game is the first person to stand up and make a statement which begins with the words "I have never....". For example, "I have never run a marathon". Remember this must be a True statement. Then if anybody in the circle has in fact done what the person said they have never done then they must take a drink. When the drinking has subsided then play moves to the person on the left of the first person to make the statement.

This game will only work if people are totally honest. However you may wish to invoke a Judge and Jury system. If there is a dispute as to whether one of the players has indeed ever done something or not, then the Jury (being all the other players) must decide and the Judge (being the person making the original statement) must dictate a penalty. Falsely taking a drink to increase your street cred, for example drinking to a statement "I have never had sex with Cindy Crawford", is to be frowned upon and severely penalised.

Fuzzy Duck

Blitz Factor 3

Does he?

How to Play:

Anyone starts a game by looking to their right and saying "Fuzzy Duck". The person to the right now continues and looks to their right also saying "Fuzzy Duck". This continues until anybody looks back at the person who as just spoken to them and asks "Duzzy?". This changes the direction and changes the words to "Ducky Fuzz". Anyone can then reverse the direction by simply asking "Duzzy?"

Anybody who messes up obviously drinks. Speed is of the essence and the no swearing rule must be strictly adhered to. Anyone who messes up with a sentence that sounds like "Fuck he does" must drink twice the usual penalty.

Quick Game

Reverse Drinking. Turn your hand through 180 degrees, pick up your beer and drink it in 'reverse hand'. If your friends haven't watched closely, challenge them to do it. If they fail to turn their hand before picking up their drinks, the results can be quite amusing.

For Amusement Only

Ibble-Dibble

Blitz Factor 3

Again where your arithmetical ability is just as important as your drinking skills you will come out looking like a spotty dog with the case of the measles, and mumbling like a complete idiot. But what the hell.

You will need a cork or a felt tip pen and plenty of beer.

How to Play:

The original game is played with a cork which has been blackened on one end by burning it with a match, but if you do not have a cork then use an indelible felt tip pen.

Everyone sits around a table and is given a number according to their position:

The host will be number one, the person to their left number 2, the next person number 3, etc. These people then identify themselves with the words Ibble-Dibble, so the host is Ibble- Dibble 1, the person to his left Ibble-Dibble 2, the next one Ibble-Dibble 3, etc.

Play then commences with the host identifying himself, saying the name of another player and identifying how many marks they have on their forehead.

These marks, or spots, are called Dibble-Ibbles, and are acquired by making a mistake. So the first statement will go something like this, "Ibble-Dibble 1 to Ibble-Dibble 4 with no Dibble-Ibbles".

That player must then respond with the name of the person who is calling them and the number of marks on their forehead, "Yes Ibble-Dibble 1 with no Dibble-Ibbles". The original player will then complete the transaction with, "Over to you Ibble-Dibble 4". Play then progresses with, in this case, Ibble-Dibble 4 taking the chair.

If you make a mistake with the name or the words, or you pause during your statement, then you must take a drink and somebody will place a Dibble-Ibble upon your forehead with the cork or pen. Play comes to a halt whilst penalties are being taken and then the player who has been penalised must try again.

There is no natural conclusion to this game so play usually ends when everybody gets so pissed that there is no continuity whatsoever

Spot

Blitz Factor 2

If the use of Ibble-Dibble and Dibble-Ibble is too difficult even at the beginning you may wish to use the words spot.

How to Play:

The opening sentence in this scenario would go, "Spot 1 to Spot 4 with no spots." Although the difficulty of Ibble-Dibble and Dibble-Ibble is removed you must be very strict about numbers proceeding and preceding the word "spot".

The "try again rule" usually works very well. However, there will come a point when one player gets into extreme difficulty and cannot manage to utter a complete correct sentence without pausing. Set a limit at say five attempts and if they still cannot get it right ask them to leave the game and go home to their mummies.

In the basic game a person who makes a mistake is given a spot on their forehead but you could allow the person who is being addressed by the sender to place the spot or mark anywhere upon the offending person. So it might go on their nose, in their ears or anywhere else where naked flesh can be found.

Drinking Games 2000

Games Directory

Bookshop Central

All of the Internet's bookshops together in one place. Save hours searching different sites and find that elusive book, and check out the cheapest prices: Visit

www.bookshopcentral.co.uk

MORE HUMOUR TITLES...

The Drinking Man's Survival Guide

Discover how to celebrate the joys of drinking... stock up on excuses to get you out of trouble, drink for free... learn to sip and save by making your own beer and wine... make recipes to eat your favourite booze... and meet the world's most amazing drinkers. *£3.99*

The Hangover Handbook & Boozer's Bible

Ever groaned, burped and cursed the morning after, as Vesuvius erupted in your stomach, a bass drummer thumped on your brain and a canary fouled its nest in your throat? Then you need these 100+ hangover remedies. There's an exclusive Hangover Ratings Chart, a Boozer's Calendar, a Hangover Clinic, and you can meet the Great Drunks of History, try the Boozer's Reading Chart, etc., etc. *£3.99*

The Beerlover's Bible *(In the shape of a beercan)*

Do you love beer? Then this is the book you have been waiting for - a tantalising brew of fascinating facts, stories and humour to help everybody enjoy their favourite fluid all the more. Discover how to... Serve beer for maximum enjoyment... Brew your own beer... Eat beer - with tasty recipes for everything from beer soup to beer sweets... Entertain with beer - whether at a barbecue or with silver service.

The Beerlover's Bible brews up a host of fascinating facts and figures that will make you a walking encyclopedia about the world's favourite drink. *£3.99*

Keep Fit With Booze

Here, at last, is the exercise programme all serious drinkers have been waiting for. If drinkers have no time to visit the gym, the gym must be taken to the drinkers.

Alco-robics has been born: a unique exercise system that can be practised easily by anyone who has ever raised a glass. No special skills are needed... simply open the book, open a bottle and get started! *£3.99*

MORE GOOD BOOKS...

The Complete Beginner's Guide to The Internet   £5.95

Everywhere you turn these days, it's Internet this, Cyberspace that and Superhighway the other. Indeed, hardly a day goes by without us being bombarded with information and reasons why you should be on the Net. But none of that is of much help in making an informed decision about joining and using the Internet.

What exactly is The Internet? Where did it come from and where is it going? And, more importantly, how can everybody take their place in this new community?

The Complete Beginner's Guide to The Internet answers all of those questions and more. On top of being an indispensable guide to the basics of Cyberspace, it is the lowest priced introduction on the market by a long way at a *surfer-friendly price.*

Complete Beginner's Guide to the World Wide Web	**£5.95**
Complete Beginner's Guide to Windows 98	**£5.95**
Complete Beginner's Guide to Word for Windows	**£5.95**
Create Your Own Website	**£5.95**
Find What You Want on the Interent	**£5.95**

Postage and handling charge:
UK - £1 for first book, and 50p for each additional book
Elsewhere - £3 for first book, and £1.50 for each additional book.

Please send me a copy of
☐ I enclose a cheque/payment made payable to 'Take That Ltd'.
☐ Please debit my Visa/Amex/Mastercard number

Signature: _____   Expiry Date: _____
Name: _____
Address: _____
_____
_____
_____ Postcode: _____

Please return to: **Take That Ltd., P.O.Box 200, Harrogate, HG1 2YR**

Please allow 14-21 days delivery. We hope to make you further exciting offers in the future. If you do not wish to receive these, please write to us at the above address.   DGames2